A Thousand Paths to Enlightenment

A Thousand Paths to
enlightenment

Sourcebooks, Inc.
Naperville, IL

David Baird

Contents

# Introduction

In these complex, stress-filled times many of us turn to extreme—often exotic—sources in the hope of gaining some enlightenment. But when we set out on the path of morality, meditation, and wisdom that we hope will lead us to nirvana, we can sometimes make our lives even *more* complicated than they were before. Worse still, we end up none the more enlightened for our pains.

Enlightenment is not a complicated and elitist club from which some are excluded. In fact, despite working perfectly well for some, there are many enlightened minds who never even attempted sitting in lotus position or chanting a mantra. Anyone who is willing to open their mind is free to pursue enlightenment. This collection of inspirational thoughts may be just the beginning of your journey.

The
Knowledge

The greatest lesson in life is to know that even fools are right sometimes.

Remember that not getting what you want is sometimes a stroke of luck.

Fools and fanatics always seem certain of themselves, wise people are full of doubts.

Wise men have something to say; fools have to say something.

Learn all the rules—
then break some.

Wise men don't need advice; fools
don't take advice.

In life there are those objects that
don't move and there are those
that you are unable to move.

It is impossible to look forward and
backward at the same time.

History is in a way our collective memory, without memory we would be demoted to the lower animals.

We love only what we do not completely possess.

Believe in love at first sight.

Learn to live a life rather than to spend a life avoiding death—life is not breath but action.

Life involves passions, faiths, doubts, and courage.

Mistakes are the dues one pays for a full life.

Freedom is a fine word when rightly understood.

Act in the living present.

There are those who are compelled to work by the sweat of their brow and are reduced to the misery of slavery, and there are those who love their work and are free and happy.

Humanity can be split into two classes of creatures: those who make great demands on themselves, piling up difficulties and duties; and those who demand nothing special of themselves, but for whom to live is to be every moment what they already are, without imposing on themselves any effort toward perfection, mere buoys that float on the waves.

**What
is man
but his
passion?**

Without passion man is a mere latent force and possibility, like the flint which awaits the shock of the iron before it can give forth its spark.

If there is a hell on earth, it is to be found in a melancholy man's heart.

Our future depends on us combining our passions with our best interests.

Peace can only come as a natural consequence of universal enlightenment.

Memorize your favorite poem.

There are those who talk about their rights, and there are those who go out and demand their rights.

You don't have to stay up nights to succeed, you have to stay awake days.

You can't propel yourself forward by patting yourself on the back.

You can fool some of the people all of the time.
You can fool all of the people some of the time.
But you can't fool all of the people all of the time.

You can't tell which way the train went just by looking at the track.

Sometimes in life the glass seems half empty, sometimes it seems half full, and sometimes the glass is twice as large as it needs to be.

You only live once, do it right and once is enough.

It may be that your whole purpose in life is simply to serve as a warning to others.

It makes no difference whether you win or you lose—that is, of course, until you lose.

It's easy to get lost in thought, especially if it's not familiar territory to you.

Just because
your doctor has
a name for your
condition
doesn't
necessarily
mean that he
knows what it is.

It is hard to make anything foolproof, because fools are so ingenious.

Keep your head and your heart going in the right direction and you won't have to worry about your feet.

Time past is time gone.

Minds are like parachutes, if they are closed they won't hold you up.

Mistakes are the stepping stones to the future.

The more sins you confess, the more books you will sell.

The most effective answer to any insult is silence.

Nobody trips over mountains. It is the little stones that cause us to stumble.

Never appeal to a man's "better nature." It's possible that he might not have one.

Success requires obsessive desire; co-ordinated thoughts, aims and actions; concentrated energy, and constant application. And with all that in place, it's easy to be successful.

The only people who don't go around talking about other people are those on ego trips.

The one who says it cannot be done should never interrupt the one who is doing it.

The only time the world beats a path to your door is usually when you are in the bathroom.

People seldom know what they want until you give them what they don't want.

The narrower the mind, the broader the tongue.

Punctuality is only satisfying if there is somebody there to appreciate it.

Confuse an approaching frown
with a smile.

Someone who thinks logically is a nice
contrast to the real world.

Some men can spend all day
walking through a forest and see
no firewood at all.

Keep a tight lead on your dogma or
it might get run over by someone
else's karma.

There are three kinds of
people you have to worry
about in life:
Those who can count.
And those who can't.

You can't travel
faster than the
speed of time
which is one
second per second.

Life is a form of
obsessive-
compulsive disorder.

There's a fine line
between courage
and foolishness.

Mankind is in trouble—there has been a shocking increase in the number of things we know nothing about.

Somewhere there's an old proverb that says just about whatever you want it to.

Imagine a life with no hypothetical situations.

Any philosopher will tell you that today is the tomorrow that you were worried about yesterday.

Why is it that whenever a piano needs to be moved everybody volunteers to carry the stool?

Virtue is in a way its own punishment.

Don't waste tears on what might have been.

At the end of the day when all is said and done, more is said than done.

We, the unwilling, led by the unknowing, are doing the impossible for the ungrateful.

In order to achieve one should work for eight hours, sleep for eight hours and do other necessary things for eight hours. The important thing here is that one doesn't try to do it all in the same eight hours.

It is impossible to simultaneously achieve presence of mind and absence of body. Although if it were possible, there would be far fewer accidents.

Worry takes just as much time as work and pays less.

All the easy problems in this life have already been solved, leaving us the tricky ones.

Children insist upon behaving just like their parents, despite the fact that one strives to teach them good manners.

As one grows older one falls for less and stands for more.

Computers are not intelligent. They only think they are.

Some things in life simply don't add up. Even computers can't solve those ones.

Sometimes it seems that the
only difference between
democracy and mob rule is
that with democracy there
is income tax to pay.

Copying from one is called plagiarism, but
if you copy from many it's called research.

Genius has its limits, stupidity has none.

Sometimes the finest
command of language is
to say nothing.

History repeats itself,
but each time the
price goes up.

If you can find a way of expressing your joy you will intensify it.

Learn to recognize when to shut your mouth before someone else tells you to.

Free advice generally costs more than any other kind.

The greatest threat towards the future is indifference.

We have become so conditioned to bad results that when something goes right the first time we swoon in astonishment.

He who hesitates is lost.

It is wiser to gain wisdom from someone else's mishaps than your own.

Nature versus science: Nature breeds better mice. Science builds better mousetraps.

Ignorance is bliss. Perhaps that's why everyone is smiling.

If you can smile when things go wrong it probably means you weren't to blame.

Feeling bad or worrying will not change the past or some future event.

I have often regretted my speech, never my silence.

An error only becomes a mistake if you refuse to correct it.

Where there is no vision there can be no achievement.

There are those who sit in uncertainty hoping to predict the future, and those who invent their futures and lead predictable lives.

We can do anything in this life that we want to provided we stick to it long enough.

There are two kinds of people—those who see life as a mountain of insurmountable problems, and those who see each day as a mountain of insurmountable opportunities.

To achieve greatly you must be prepared to fail greatly.

In life, as in war, pick battles big enough to matter, but small enough to win.

Don't let fear stop you.

We may want what we want when we want it but more often we get what we get when we get it.

It's not what they take away from you that counts, it's what you choose to do with what you have left.

With love and a bit of patience there is nothing that is totally impossible.

Any road will take you nowhere if that's where you're going.

Remember the good—
the bad will remember you.

Great mistakes usually
take quite an amount of skill
to achieve.

Simplicity is complex.

We have the right of existence and the right of self-determination.

When intellectuals are let loose on art the result is interpretation.

**Experience is that
marvellous thing that
enables you to recognize
a mistake when you
make it again.**

The very fact we exist makes it impossible to avoid affecting others positively and negatively.

Man is what he believes.

Of the universal mind each man is but one more incarnation.

To accept what you are is to be content, and there is no wealth to compare with contentment.

If we can go deep into ourselves we will find we possess exactly what it is we desire.

If you are constantly attempting to justify your own existence to yourself, through your own efforts then you are your own slave.

It is better to tell a painful truth than to lie.

Determine to spend your life engaged in constant, eager observation and you will be rewarded through enlightenment.

Feeling bad with a clear conscience is better than feeling good with a bad conscience.

Eight words that can help make life run much more smoothly: "You know…you may very well be right."

In life we either follow paths or make trails.

There is success and there is the appearance of success.

Footprints on the sands of time weren't created by those sitting down.

We have done so much, for so long, with so little, we are now qualified to do anything with nothing.

Sharing

The enlightened do not see life in black and white.

Everyone has an inalienable right to their own thoughts.

In many cases it is easier to love humanity than to love your neighbor.

People hate those who make them feel their own inferiority.

Make it your aim to live honestly, injure no one, and give every person their due.

Regard all men as equal.

For the enlightened there are no classes—only individuals.

The world needs closer contact and better understanding between individuals and communities—peace can only come as a consequence of universal enlightenment.

To live is
to think.

A man who
does not think
for himself
does not think
at all.

Live and
let live.

There are only two kinds of immoral conduct. The first is due to indifference, thoughtlessness and failure to reflect upon what is for the common good. The second is represented by the deliberate refusal, after reflection, to follow the light when seen.

Love is the strongest and deepest element in all our lives; it is the harbinger of hope, of joy, of ecstasy; it defies all laws and all conventions; it is the freest, and the most powerful shaper of human destiny.

The most important thing in life is to be capable of loving.

The first and highest law must be the love of humanity.

Love makes its center the axis of the universal whole. Love aims at unity.

In the development of mankind as a whole, just as in individuals, love alone acts as the civilizing factor in the sense that it brings a change from egoism to altruism.

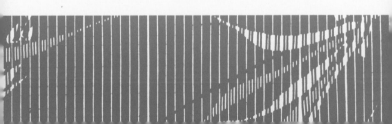

The real friend is another self.

Love is the only force capable of transforming an enemy into a friend.

Real friends reserve nothing.

Each friend represents a world in us, a world not born until they arrive.

The finest feelings known to humanity: conjugal love and paternal affection.

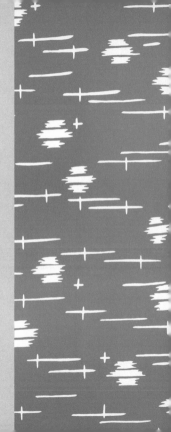

Love thy neighbor.

The supreme happiness of life is the conviction that we are loved.

Love is the strongest force the world possesses, yet it is also the most humbling.

The great tragedy of life is not that men perish, but that they cease to love.

An ounce of love is worth a pound of knowledge.

To set a price on love is to devalue the priceless.

Seek not every quality in one individual.

Without a true friend a person cannot discern the errors of their own actions.

We fluctuate long between love and hatred before we arrive at tranquillity.

No man
is useless
while
he is a
friend.

When you say, "I love you," mean it.

They who have never loved,
have never lived.

Where there is love there are miracles.

Hatred paralyses life; love releases it.

Hatred confuses life; love harmonizes it.

Hatred darkens life; love illuminates it.

The intention makes the crime.

They who allow oppression share the crime.

You cannot shake hands with a clenched fist.

Why is it that friends make the worst enemies?

They who never trust themselves never trust anyone.

Greater understanding increases the capacity for tolerance.

Share your knowledge. It is a way to achieve immortality.

My own mind is my own church.

The intention makes the lie, not the words.

The brightest flashes in the world of thought are incomplete until they have been proved to have their counterpart in the world of fact.

Tact is the ability to describe others as they see themselves.

Honesty is
the first
chapter of
the book of
wisdom.

The cruellest
lies are often
told in
silence.

Kindness is greater than law.

Do not judge your friend until you stand in his place.

Morality is the observance of the rights of others.

Do not do to your neighbor that which you would not suffer from him.

He who sows courtesy reaps friendship, and he who plants kindness gathers love.

To love is virtually to know; to know is not virtually to love.

Real friends are those who, when you've made a fool of yourself, don't feel that you've done a permanent job.

Remember that the best relationship is the one where your love for each other is greater than your need for each other.

The most important element in any home is a loving atmosphere.

Do all you can to create a tranquil harmonious home.

A little dispute shouldn't be allowed to injure a great friendship.

If someone asks you a question that you don't feel you want to answer, smile and ask, "Why do you want to know?"

The person who is only
known through their partner
is not known.

Let humanity be your guide.

Learn to love deeply and
passionately. This way you
might get hurt, but it's the only
way to really live life to the full.

Only by accepting our actions can we make ourselves and our lives whole. We are all responsible for what we have done and for those we have influenced.

If in doubt whether an action would be good or bad, picture yourself in the position of those whom it will affect, and think again.

When faced with the choice between two evils, postpone choice.

As human beings we are held together only by the strength of our word.

Loneliness and the feeling of being unwanted can be devastating. We can take these feelings away from others simply by being generous with our time and compassion.

The level of mankind's understanding corresponds directly to the extent of the freedom of inquiry which is held out to him.

If the mind of man is to be free, then his philosophy, his ideology and his beliefs must all be placed safely out of the reach of government.

Governments depend on criticism in order to govern appropriately. Without it they would be lost.

Who is to watch the watchers?

Placing a
restraint
upon
opinion is
like trying
to limit the
senses of
taste or
smell.

We must try not to be drawn into the game of deceiving the deceivers.

Anyone who believes they have converted a person simply because they have silenced them is badly mistaken.

Education is a gift that benefits all.

Freedom only exists if you allow yourself to take the time to be free.

We must not only stand up for the rights of the 1,000 who are of one opinion—we must also stand up for the rights of the solitary figure who stands against that opinion.

**The basis of all human behavior
must be the quest to retain one's
own dignity without intruding on
the liberty of others.**

Enlightenment is not only
for individuals.

Each generation leaves behind them unfinished challenges for the next generation, and education is the best thing we can give them to protect themselves with.

Anything which attempts
to crush individuality
is despotism.

Freedom is like farming the land—to reap its harvest one must be prepared to nurture it and put up with the often exhausting burden of supporting it.

The greatest menace to
enlightenment is inertia.

Evil will triumph if the good
do nothing.

Standing still means
going backwards.

The freedom of the individual on the other side of the world is our freedom too.

We can never be truly free while there is another human being in slavery.

It is far nobler to die on one's feet than to live on one's knees.

Truth has dirty hands.

Enlightenment comes only with responsibility.

Enlightenment is activity.

Enlightenment is the power to argue freely according to your conscience.

Freedom of
expression
is the well that
sustains civilization.

Knowledge is the single most essential right of mankind.

Disapprove of what is said by all means but always defend the right to say it.

There is nothing nobler than humanity.

The earth is the
common property of
the human race, and
of every living thing.

Always look for points of agreement rather than argument.

Learn to know yourself before you presume to know another.

Precedent is not to be relied upon.

The enlightened person will listen and learn more from those who are in opposition than from those whose sole aim is to please.

It is impossible to know all the answers, content yourself with knowing some of the questions.

It is not enough to follow the same path as the wise, you must seek what they sought.

Sometimes it is important not to think, but to feel.

Experience what it is to live without guilt and without desire.

With every answer
come two new
questions.

If you have tried, then that is enough.

Make your compassion infinite.

Neither look down on, or up to, others.

The person we need the most protection from, and who can do us the most damage, is ourself.

If you refuse to open the door that leads to enlightenment nobody else can do it for you.

**Have respect for yourself;
find respect for others;
take responsibility for all
your actions.**

They who do not think for themselves
do not think at all.

Focus on:
the sanctity of human life,
the dignity of humankind,
the right of every human being
to freedom and well-being.

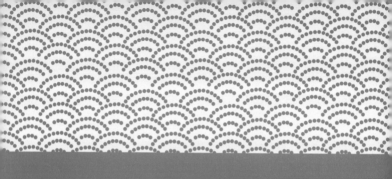

Endeavour to live each day that dawns
as if it were going to be your last.

Enlightenment is blind to
external appearances.

Forgiveness is not an occasional act; it is a permanent attitude.

You can't understand another person until you allow yourself to step in their shoes.

Learn to share, it is a way of doubling the good and halving the bad.

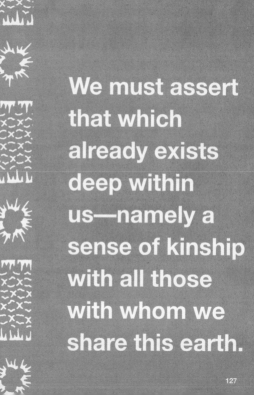

We must assert that which already exists deep within us—namely a sense of kinship with all those with whom we share this earth.

Enlightenment is
not the end, it is
simply the means
to the end.

Intentions

Never interrupt
when you are being
flattered.

In disagreements with loved ones, deal with the current situation. Don't bring up the past.

Where there is a feast of words there is often a famine of wisdom.

The wise man has long ears and a short tongue.

Remember that silence is sometimes the best answer.

The beginning of wisdom is to call things by their true names.

It is a brave man that calls everything by its right name.

It is not the answer that enlightens, but the question.

Never use two words when one will do.

Eating words has never given anyone indigestion.

"No comment" is a splendid expression.

A bore is a person who opens his mouth and puts his feats in it.

It is easier to talk than to hold one's tongue.

He who says what he likes will hear what he does not like.

Speak the truth and shame the devil.

If you do not tell the truth about yourself you cannot tell it about other people.

Consider before contradicting.

Never laugh at anyone's dreams.

When you say, "I'm sorry," look the person in the eye and make sure they realize you mean it.

Don't judge people by their relatives, judge them by their friends.

Perhaps we should invent a word
for old friends who have just met.

A friend is an ally in an
uncertain world.

Compromise does not
mean cowardice.

Act so that it will give your friends
no occasion for regret and your
foes no cause for joy.

Money is no substitute for ideas.

The desire for security is the barrier that has stood against many a great and noble enterprise.

Anyone entrusted with power must be animated with the love of truth and virtue, no matter whether he be a prince, or one of the people.

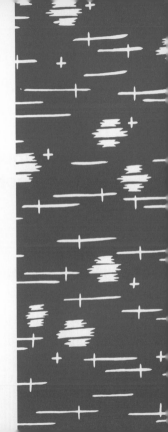

Whoever is careless with the truth in small things cannot be trusted with important matters.

All who deliberate on controversial matters, should be free from hate, friendship, anger, and pity.

Life is filled with wondrous questions and mediocre answers.

Do not judge others by stricter standards than you set for yourself.

The task of history is to establish the truth.

History is the nightmare that we must wake from.

Those who cannot remember the past are condemned to repeat it.

In this world nothing is certain except the past.

We speak about creation as if it were over. Creation is taking place every moment of our lives.

He who works for eternity counts not time.

Truth changes depending on your perspective.

More people are taken in by hope than by cunning.

Those who feed on hope exist but do not live.

Do not speak of your life only in the future tense.

Hope for nothing, fear nothing, be free.

Faith is our
awareness of
something greater
than ourselves, to
which we are
connected.

Faith is an
insurance policy
we underwrite
with our lives.

Nothing can close off the mind and imagination more securely than ignorance.

No soul is desolate as long as there is a human being for whom it can feel trust and reverence.

Cherish your dreams, but don't let them distract you from the important business of living.

**To know, to think, to dream.
That is everything.**

Deny nothingness.

**The greatest thing in the world is for
a man to know how to be himself.
And to be satisfied with that.**

There are as many routes to enlightenment as there are stars in the night sky.

Enlightenment is simplicity of life and elevation of purpose.

Allow yourself the freedom to dream, that is everything.

Set your standards high, but not impossibly so.

Have the courage to aspire to a better state of being.

Our ideals, hopes, and desires are what determine our future.

Believe in yourself, and accept yourself for who you are.

Keep your eyes on the stars, but keep your feet on the ground.

Power is nothing more than a means to an end.

There is nothing of which we are so fond, and which we are so careless with, as life.

Never lose sight of your goal—it helps if you know what you are aiming for.

The easiest task for mankind is to deceive himself. It seems we are ever willing to believe what we wish to be true.

The two most dangerous foes of human happiness are pain and boredom.

Boredom is the catalyst to many of the world's sins.

Inhibition does not come naturally—it must be learned.

Activity is the antidote to boredom.

No one ever became extremely wicked at the drop of a hat.

We are our own worst enemy.

It is easier to fight for principles than to live up to them.

As a rule mankind selects to disbelieve all facts and theories for which he has no use.

To err is human, to forgive is divine.

We grow old the moment we stop learning. The secret of eternal youth is to keep learning.

It is far better to prevent crimes than to punish them.

If you think that you have learned all there is to learn, then you haven't even started.

There are no short cuts to enlightenment.

It is thinking that makes us what we truly are.

We must find out truth for ourselves, and in ourselves.

Education is a weapon whose effect depends on who holds it in his hands and at whom it is aimed.

Education is a process of living and not a preparation for future living.

Reason is our highest gift, and that which is most under-used.

Reason means facing life, and its facts—pleasant or otherwise.

Only through reason can we expect to gain any kind of understanding of the problems that face us.

Therè is no education like adversity.

We must learn from the past, prepare for the future, and live in the present.

To perceive is to suffer.

Do not avoid evil only because you fear punishment and do good only because you hope for a reward.

Promises are issued according to our hopes, but our performance is judged according to our fears.

Anxiety is a thin stream of fear trickling through the mind. If encouraged, it cuts a channel into which all other thoughts are drained.

A little nonsense now and then is cherished by the wisest men.

Truth fears no questions.

Unless you attempt something beyond what you have already mastered, you will never grow.

If you can learn to laugh at yourself you will never cease to be amused.

Procrastination is still procrastination even if you put it off right away.

You can explain things to people but you can't do the understanding for them.

Enlightenment may not set you on the right path, but it allows you to read the signpost.

He who knows little
quickly tells it.

Italian proverb

**You're never too old to learn
something stupid.**

Be swift to praise and slow to criticize.

Sometimes we can't hear opportunity when it knocks on the front door because temptation is persistently banging on the back door.

Everybody will accept your idea much more readily if you tell them that somebody famous said it first.

What we cannot speak about we must pass over in silence.

Use too many sweet words and you may have to eat them.

If you don't know where you're going, any road will do.

Enough research will support any theory.

There can't be a crisis today, the schedule is already full.

Our worst enemy is fear of change.

If there is such a thing as free speech why are telephone bills so high?

Beware of the man who knows
the answer before he understands
the question.

Don't spend so much time worrying
about tomorrow that you forget
about today.

A conceited person never gets anywhere because they think they are already there.

Never cut what can be untied.

Laws, like the spider's web, catch the fly and let the hawk go free.

People can't change truth—truth changes people.

What's the meaning of words when there's nothing to say?

Experience is something you don't get until just after the moment you need it.

Make sure that you are safely across the river before you start calling the crocodiles names.

The nail that sticks out is hammered down.

Japanese proverb

The squeaky wheel gets the grease.

Speak less, act more.

Think twice before you speak, once uttered, there is no calling back a hasty word.

Words, cruelly used, are the most damaging of weapons.

A kind word is never forgotten.

Learn to recognize when to speak and when to stay silent.

Learn to love silence.

When you don't know what to say, say nothing.

Actions

Begin at once to live, and count each separate day as a separate life.

Be gentle with the earth.

Excellence is the best deterrent to racism and sexism.

You can make more friends in two weeks by being interested in other people than you can in two years by trying to get other people interested in you.

If you want to gather honey, don't kick over the beehive.

Neither love too much, nor hate in the same extreme.

Always act as if you were seen.

That which is necessary is never a risk.

Make reason your guide.

In the practical use of the intellect, forgetting is as important as remembering.

As well as learning to see, learn also not to see what is not.

Our life is what our actions make it.

Wisdom is acquired by an active mind.

Genius means little more than the faculty of perceiving in an unhabitual way.

Genius is a conquering of chaos and mystery.

Ignorance is not bliss,
it is oblivion.

**Have the courage
to be wise.**

Never consider anything as profitable which compels you to break a promise or to lose your self-respect.

Do nothing against your conscience.

Though strong medicines be nauseous to the taste, they are good for the disease; though candid advice may be unpleasant to hear, it is profitable for one's conduct.

Truth is a question of the reconciling and combining of opposites, and very few have minds sufficiently capacious and impartial to make the correct judgements.

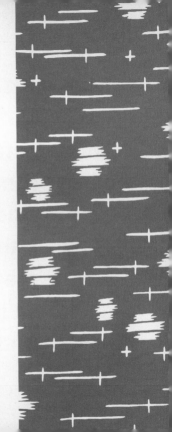

True opinions can prevail only if the facts to which they refer are known.

When the facts are fairly and honestly presented, truth will take care of itself.

Plain and unvarnished are the words of truth.

Nothing is safe that does not bear discussion and publicity.

The mission of the intellect is to guide mankind over the sea of error to the safe haven of truth.

We can only find the truth for ourselves.

The truth will not always be palatable, but without it there can be no progress.

As a rule we are prone to disbelieve all facts and theories for which we have no use.

Scepticism is the first step toward truth.

One single well-established fact, clearly irreconcilable with a doctrine, is sufficient to prove that it is false.

Truth does not change because it is, or is not believed by the majority of the people.

A new truth does
not triumph by
convincing its
opponents and
making them see
the light,
but rather because
its opponents
eventually die out,
and a new
generation grows
up that
is familiar with it.

Adversity is the first step on the path to truth.

Enlightenment comes only through the realization of the greater truths.

Every definition is dangerous.

Seek to know the truth, but above all, love truth.

It does not require many words to speak the truth.

Confession is the next best thing to innocence.

Truth is not only violated by falsehood; it is outraged by silence.

An unexciting truth may be eclipsed by a thrilling lie.

An ability to see the truth in small, as well as great, things is the only way to progress towards enlightenment.

Self-confidence means finding your inner sanctuary, and fully realizing the infinite support that it provides.

Enlightenment must come little by little—or it will overwhelm us.

Just do what you do best. It is the purpose for which you were made.

When you have developed the ability to do the small jobs well, greater jobs will come to you.

There are people living in a dream world, and people living in the real world, and people who don't know the difference.

When your horse is running well, don't stop to feed him sugar.

When faced with a difficult task, say to yourself others have done this before me.

The demand for ability always outstrips the supply of ability.

As we advance in life we learn the limits of our abilities.

Work is a presentation of our capabilities.

Knowing how to hide your ability takes great skill.

If you don't know
your limits, then you
don't know the
heights of what you
can achieve.

Good fortune and good sense seldom come in the same package.

With enlightenment comes the realization that we do not have a natural longing to do those things for which we have no ability.

When one must, one can.

Yiddish proverb

Spend less time analysing the things you don't have and create more time to enjoy those things you do have.

Behind every able man, there are always other able men.

Chinese proverb

Count all your failures and you will show a loss. Count all your assets and you will always show a profit.

Celebrate your ability to motivate yourself to do whatever is necessary.

Be bold and persistent in experimentation—accepting failure and moving on is infinitely more enlightening than admitting defeat and giving up.

Genius is
the child
of skill
and love
working
together in
harmony.

Everybody has some form of ability. Enlightenment leads some to choose to use it.

Ability is a poor man's wealth.

You are the only person on
earth who can use your ability.

Learn to love what you do,
or stop.

It is ten times harder to command the ear than to catch the eye.

Don't just stand there—do something.

When your dreams turn to dust, vacuum.

Take care that the face that looks out from the mirror in the morning is a pleasant face. You may not see it again during the day, but others will.

If you put a low value upon yourself, rest assured that the world will not raise your price.

Choose to take control of your own life. If you don't, someone else will.

The art of living is knowing to be ready at any time for an unseen attack.

The life that is most useful to us will also be the most agreeable.

Sometimes it is better to act before thinking, otherwise the shark will consume us while we ponder its lifestyle.

There will always be those who, no matter what has happened, insist on behaving as though nothing had.

We are always keen to learn, although few like being taught.

We always remember the things said to us in anger, but remember also those things said in love and friendship.

If you have an important point to make, don't try to be subtle or clever.

It is a mistake to look too far ahead. Only one link in the chain of destiny can be handled at a time.

A fanatic is one who can't change his mind and won't change the subject.

Politics is like war, and just as dangerous. In war you can only be killed once, but in politics it can happen over and over again.

Everything should be made as simple as possible, but not simpler.

Anyone who has never made a mistake has never tried anything new.

Never think of the future. It comes soon enough.

The difference between what the most and the least learned people know is trivial in relation to that which is unknown.

A fabulous experience that lasts for a day can seem but a moment, but hit your thumb with a hammer and that moment seems longer than a day. That is relativity.

An intellectual is one who takes more words than necessary to tell more than they know.

Failure is a great opportunity to begin again more intelligently.

Whether you think you can or think you can't—you are probably right.

The only real security in this world is a reserve of knowledge, experience, and ability.

Everyone it seems has courage enough to bear the misfortunes, and wisdom enough to manage the affairs, of their neighbour.

Any fool can criticize and most fools do.

Wealth is not his who has it but his who enjoys it.

Creditors have better memories than debtors.

From those to whom much is given, much is required.

Nothing in the world is more dangerous than sincere ignorance and conscientious stupidity.

Use your time creatively.

Darkness cannot drive out darkness; only light can do that. Hate cannot drive out hate.

The ultimate measure of a man is not where he stands in moments of comfort and convenience, but where he stands at times of challenge and controversy.

Force is all-conquering, but its victories are short-lived.

Most people can stand adversity, but if you want to test someone's character, give them power.

The future comes but one day at a time.

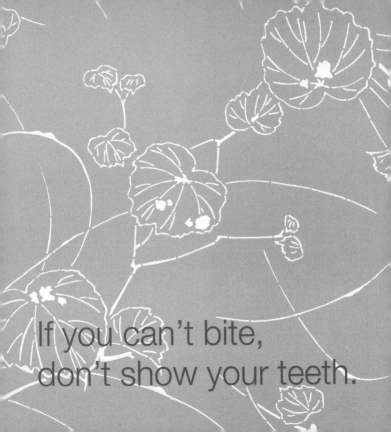

If you can't bite,
don't show your teeth.

He that does not ask will never get a bargain.

They who know little,
tell it quickly.

If you bow at all, bow low.

If you must play, decide on three things at the start: the rules of the game, the stakes, and the quitting time.

In order to command respect, you must first respect yourself.

Self-respect is the hardest to win.

If you would be wealthy, think of saving as well as getting.

It is easier to pull down than to build up.

It is not enough to aim; you must hit.

For the enlightened, the journey is the reward.

Let him make use of instinct who cannot make use of reason.

Learn to recognize your talents, don't hide them. What's a sundial in the shade?

The enlightened man will be known by his actions.

A clear and unclouded mind is capable of holding the most.

Actions, carefully considered, speak louder than words, even if they are shouted.

If you have health you have hope; and if you have hope, you have everything.

Do not rely on the opinion of others to judge your own morality.

He who would leap far must first take a long run.

Once you are outside your door, the hardest part of the journey is behind you.

239

Right actions depend on right thinking. Right thinking depends on knowing what is true.

Lifewish

Mind your own business.

Judge your success by what you had to give up in order to get it.

Smile when picking up the phone—the caller will hear it in your voice.

When you realize that you've made a mistake, take immediate steps to correct it.

Remember that great love and great achievements involve great risk.

It is neither wealth
nor splendour, but
tranquillity and
occupation, that
gives happiness.
Thomas Jefferson

In disagreements, fight fairly. That is more important than to win.

Give people more than they expect and do it cheerfully.

It is impossible to make anything foolproof because fools are so ingenious.

Nothing that is worth having ever comes except as a result of hard work.

You'd better decide what you're willing to forfeit in order to get what you want because great careers don't come without sacrifice.

The price of greatness is responsibility.

It is better to lead by example than by decree.

Do not preach your beliefs, if they are sincere they will be clear enough in your actions.

A man's own natural duty, even if it seems imperfectly done, is better than work not naturally his own, even if it is well performed.

To die for an idea is a pretty high price to pay for conjecture.

Every idea is a source of life and light which animates and illuminates words, facts, examples and emotions which are dead and dark without them.

Misanthropists and those who hate ideas are united in their ignorance of the world.

All erroneous ideas would perish of their own accord if expressed clearly.

Believe in yourself, and accept yourself for who you are. If you are satisfied with yourself, you have pleased the sternest judge.

Every day, in every way, strive to be better.

Temper your fears with the knowledge that you always have the capacity to improve.

If you think you can't then you can't. If you think you can you might just be able to.

The chief happiness for a man is to be what he is.

A person's character is their fate.

Sin isn't the breaking of divine commandments. It is the breaking of one's own integrity.

He who hates vice, loves mankind.

The moral sense of conscience is by far the most important and most noble attribute of man.

The greatest sin is to fail to recognize the humanity of others.

A man must first despise himself, and then others will despise him.

Only once you know yourself, can you presume to know another.

Most powerful is he who has himself in his own power.

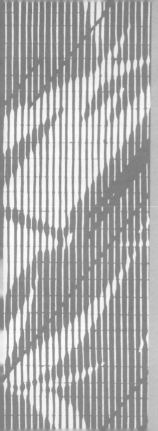

He who can govern his own anger is an extraordinary person.

Heroism is the dazzling and glorious concentration of courage.

The lack of wealth is easily repaired but the poverty of the soul is irreplaceable.

Master anger—it is your enemy.

To know men is to be wise, to know oneself is to be illuminated. To conquer men is to have strength, to conquer oneself is to be stronger still.
And to know when you have enough is to be rich.

All the miseries of mankind come from one thing, not knowing how to be alone.

The great man does not think beforehand of his words that they may be sincere, nor of his actions that they may be resolute; he simply speaks and does what is right.

When you begin to doubt that there is such a thing as a miracle, consider your mind.

Enlightenment in its essence, is the art of seeing into the nature of one's own being.

The psyche is distinctly more complicated and inaccessible than the body. It is that which comes into existence only when we become conscious of it.

Nothing can be brought to an end in the unconscious; nothing is past or forgotten.

The dream is a disguised fulfillment of a suppressed wish.

We stumble and fall constantly even when we are most enlightened. But when we are in true spiritual darkness, we do not even know that we have fallen.

If the doors of perception were cleansed, then everything would appear to man as it is, infinite.

Perceive the significance of the small things of the world.

To guard what is soft and vulnerable is the secret of strength.

An enlightened mind is always open.

The desire of one man to live off the fruits of another's labor is the central flaw of human nature.

Poverty is the mother of crime.

To live in fear of death is many times to die.

We are all in a race for dear life: that is to say, we are fugitives from death.

Everyone desires to live long,
but no one wishes to be old.

**When it happens, nothing is
more of a surprise to a
person than old age.**

Old age, to the unenlightened,
is winter; to the enlightened,
it is harvest time.

The great tragedy of life is not that men perish, but that they cease to love.

Though lovers may be lost, love shall not.

Only the dead never change their opinions.

Work is what gives structure to our lives—see it as an opportunity, not a curse.

Money is the great enabler.

Money is the cause of good things to a good man and bad things to a bad man.

Does a man think differently if he is in a palace or in a hut?

It is not he who has little, but he who desires more, that is poor.

A desire for property is one of the elements of our nature.

Fortune helps the bold.

We are all the hostages of fortune, but that doesn't mean we are powerless to change our destiny.

The greatest fruit of self-sufficiency is freedom.

He who knows how to be poor knows everything.

Property given away to friends is the only kind that will always be yours.

He who knows eternity is called enlightened.

It is not the answer or the question that enlightens, but the way of getting to the answer.

Non-co-operation with evil is as much a duty as co-operation with good.

Before enlightenment the only things we know are what we see, feel, hear, taste, and smell.

All men are born good. It is the act of living that corrupts us.

The evil life is really the thoughtless life.

We are all our own redeemer.

Evil can no more
be charged upon
God than darkness
can be charged
on the sun.

It is extreme evil to depart from the company of the living before you die.

We are our own worst enemy and our own best friend.

Seeing is believing—but don't believe all you see.

You grow up the day you have your first real laugh, at yourself.

The fragrance always stays in the hand that gives the rose.

The show must go on, whether you choose to play a part or not.

Our faith in the present dies out long before our faith in the future.

The secret of getting ahead is simply to get started.

Justice is better than chivalry if we can't have both.

Change the way you live your life now if you are going to have regrets.

Alter the difficulties or you alter yourself.

If we had no winter, the spring would not be so pleasant.

A committee takes hours to put into minutes what can be done in seconds.

Prejudices are difficult to eradicate from an uneducated heart.

Look twice before you leap.

Everything goes away eventually.

Common sense is the most under-employed talent.

Lonely are the rich.

Adventure is worthwhile in itself.

Things are rarely as good as they seem beforehand.

Big doesn't necessarily mean better.

Sunflowers aren't necessarily better than daisies.

Nobody really knows how much the heart can hold.

You don't have to have fought in a war to love peace.

Take your work seriously, but never yourself.

There are two kinds of people: those who do the work and those who take the credit. In the first group there is far less competition.

Increased stress is the price that must be payed for increased opportunity.

Advice is what we ask for when we already know the answer but wish we didn't.

Security does not exist in nature.

The only thing that makes life possible is not knowing what comes next.

The price you paid to get what you used to want is what you have become.

Govern the clock, do not be governed by it.

If you spend your life with your nose stuck to the grindstone all you'll end up with is a sore nose.

Life's under no obligation to give us what we expect.

Life is what we make it.

A computer can make as many mistakes in a few seconds as a team of men working for decades.

Don't be afraid your life will end; be afraid that it will never begin.

Winning may not be everything, but losing has little to recommend it.

Enlightenment begins where fear ends.

Some people dream of success, while others wake up and work hard at it.

The Quest

Let yesterday go, seize today, and put as little trust as you can in tomorrow.

Sometimes it is good to go someplace you've never been before.

Always read between the lines.

If you lose, make sure you don't lose the lesson too.

We shrug off miracles and then spend our lives trying to turn water into wine.

Prizes easily won are often not worth winning.

It is better to lose against a good opponent than to win against a poor one.

If you are going to dream anyway, you might as well dream big.

Most of the important things in the world have been accomplished by people who have kept on trying when there seemed to be no help at all.

An angry voice gets nowhere.
Voice your anger through
reasoned argument.

Eliminate the negative, accentuate the positive.

First ask yourself: "What is the worst
that can happen?" Then prepare to
accept it. Then proceed to improve on
the worst.

The enlightened mind does not allow emotion to trample reason.

To suppress a moment of anger may prevent many days of sorrow.

No one knows what it is that they can and cannot do until they try.

There are many wonderful things to be done, and only you can do them.

Life is about doing things, not dreaming about things.

It is often the smallest actions that have the greatest impact.

The time is always ripe to do right.

Whatever you can do, or dream you can, begin it.

Dare to take an enlightened view—it demands more, but the rewards are greater.

Do not be reckless in your conduct with others, if you respect yourself you will respect others.

He begins to die, that quits his desire.

We are the custodians of our life's meaning.

The significance of our lives derives from our own wisdom and courage.

As long as there is the rhythm of day and night, winter and summer, we will continue to dream, to believe in being saved. The idea of being renewed is part of the cycle.

Do not reason away your vision.

Salvation is a process that begins on earth and ends in eternity.

What is most contrary to salvation is not sin but habit.

The process of enlightenment can only come from within.

Strive always to see things as they really are, this is the beginning of enlightenment.

A little rebellion now and again is a good thing.

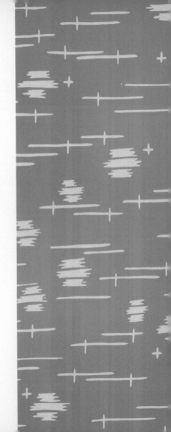

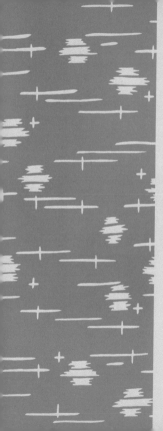

Do you love your life
enough to change it?

There is no
greater curse
than the lack of
contentment.

All people are a
single nation.

To recognize what it is that you want is the first step to getting it.

The brightest flashes of thought are incomplete until they have been proved to have their counterpart in the world of fact.

Effort without direction is wasted energy.

The beginning of
enlightenment is to
understand that you
know nothing.

No one can be a great thinker who does not follow their intellect to whatever conclusions it may lead.

Only we can discover the truth
for ourselves.

**What hope is there when people,
even in front of the evidence, turn
their head?**

Lying is an elementary means of
self-defence.

The worst person to deceive is oneself.

The most deadly lies are those that you tell to yourself.

Morality is the observance of the rights of others.

When you stop looking you stop learning.

A man is truly ethical only when he obeys the compulsion to help all life he is able to assist, and shrinks from injuring anything that lives.

The only obligation which you have the right to assume is to use your mind to its full capacity.

It is well that war is so terrible, otherwise we would grow too fond of it.

It is not dying for your country that wins wars; it is killing others so that they might die for theirs that does so.

When war is declared, truth is the
first casualty.

Mankind must put an end to
war or war will put an end
to mankind.

No nation is rich enough to pay for both
war and education.

Since wars begin in the minds of men, it is in the minds of men that the defence of peace must be constructed.

If you must, strike your blow only as a matter of necessity, not from a wish for mastery.

Supreme excellence consists in breaking the enemy's resistance without fighting.

Never ask others to do what you must do for yourself.

One must know oneself. If this does not serve to discover truth, it at least serves as a rule of life.

Respect the rights of everyone, especially yourself.

You can only be one person so decide who it is that you want to be.

The only real revolution is in the enlightenment of the mind and the improvement of the character.

Time gives good advice.

Enlighten the people
generally, and tyranny and
oppressions of body and
mind will vanish like evil
spirits at the dawn of day.

Thomas Jefferson

To change and to change for the better are two different things.

To know and to act are one and the same.

To know the road ahead, ask those coming back.

To own is to fear.

To the good listener, half a word is enough.

To want to forget something is to remember it.

The tongue ever turns to the aching tooth.

Travelers from afar can lie with impunity.

A tree never hits an automobile except in self-defence.

Vision without action is a daydream. Action without vision is a nightmare.

Use power to curb power.

Soft words win hard arguments.

Turn your face to the sun and the shadows will fall behind you.

Visits always give pleasure, if not the arrival, the departure.

Wait until it is night before saying that it has been a fine day.

We are usually the best men when in the worst health.

We do not inherit
the earth from our
ancestors;
we borrow it from
our children.

We only know the worth of a thing
when we have lost it.

We never know the worth of
water till the well is dry.

What can't be cured, must be endured.

Never underestimate anyone,
it is the most dangerous form
of arrogance.

What the heart thinks, the tongue speaks.

What the people want to believe is called the truth.

What was hard to endure is sweet to recall.

If you
don't see
it with
your eyes,
don't
invent it
with your
mouth.

What you give you get, ten times over.

When a blind man carries a lame man, both go forward.

When a thing is done, advice comes too late.

When you feel anger rising, think of the consequences and count to ten.

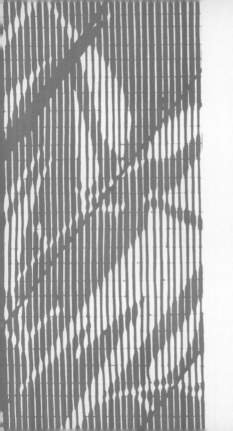

When a proud man hears another praised, he feels himself injured.

When fire and water are at war, it is the fire that loses.

If there is no enemy within, the enemies outside cannot hurt you.

When friends ask, there is no tomorrow.

When two quarrel, both are
to blame.

If you can't get what you want, you
must learn to want what you get—
or go without.

When you go to buy, use your eyes,
not your ears.

When you have no choice,
mobilize the spirit of courage.

**Whoever gossips to you
will gossip about you.**

Spanish proverb

Wherever you decide to go, go
with all your heart.

Where the river is deepest it makes least noise.

Whoever lies for you will lie against you.

Energy is man's most precious commodity, to waste it is unforgivable.

With money in your pocket you are wise, you are handsome, and you sing well too.

With time and patience the mulberry leaf becomes a silk gown.

Words must be weighed, not counted.

Everyone has their own growing, no matter how tall their grandfather was.

Make your own choices, then you will only have yourself to blame if things go wrong.

If you don't know how to do something, you don't know how to do it with a computer.

Don't be diverted from your purpose, if you were sure enough to start, be sure enough to finish.

Salvation is not about putting a man into heaven, but putting heaven into man.

Make learning your reason
for living.

**A job well done is time
well spent.**

You'll never find it if you don't
know what you're looking for.

The most
difficult
part of any
journey is
deciding
on the
destination.

Like the actor on the stage, we must play our part and say our lines whether there are seven in the audience or seven hundred.

Enlightenment is the only true way to freedom.

There is only one person whom you can trust to have your best interests at heart all the time, and that is yourself.

What may be done at any time will be done at no time.

Don't spend so long thinking about where you're going that you forget where you are.

The answer is: there is no answer.

Be sure that you recognize
what it is you were looking
for when you find it.

Attitude

Remember that your character is your destiny.

One is never old until one thinks old.

No one can give orders to love.

Our best thoughts come from others.

Ralph Waldo Emerson

One must not lose desires. They stimulate creativity, love, and long life.

Passion is the wind which fills the sails of the vessel; sometimes they sink it, but without them it would be impossible to make way.

By annihilating the desires, you annihilate the mind. Every man without passions has within him no principle of action, nor motive to act.

The great man is he who does not lose his child's heart.

People seek happiness and joy, but will often settle for pleasure.

When we never live but hope to live, and are always hoping to be happy, it is inevitable that we will never be so.

Spend some time alone.

Never take anything for granted.

Benjamin Disraeli

Very little is needed to make a happy life.

There is no wealth but life.

Knowledge if it does not determine action is dead to us.

Never give advice unless you are asked for it.

The greatest wealth is to live content with little, for there is never want where the mind is satisfied.

Ideas have to be wedded to action.

You gain strength, courage and confidence from every experience which makes you stop, look fear in the face, and do the thing which you think you cannot do.

Compromise does not mean cowardice.

No man creates from reason but from necessity.

Ability may get you to the top, but it takes character to stay there.

Loneliness, poverty, and pain make a mockery of what human life should be.

Man drags man down, or man lifts man up.

We all have strength enough to endure
the misfortune of others.

Humanity unites us.

A child's mind knows no limit to their
own will, and it is the only reality to
them. Like the artist, they go forth to
creation, gloriously alone.

Solitude vivifies, isolation kills.

Solitude is the furnace of transformation.

Natural abilities are like natural plants; they need pruning by study.

Francis Bacon

Some are full of promise, some just make promises.

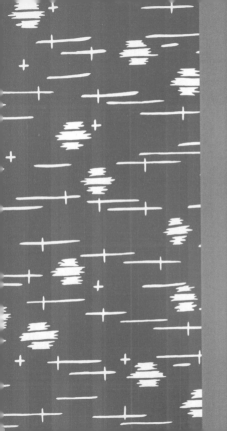

That life is worth living is the most necessary of assumptions.

One can acquire everything in solitude— except character.

Chaos breeds life when order breeds habit.

He that studies books will know how things ought to be; he that studies men will know how things are.

We are always getting ready to live, but never living.

Life is short; live it up.

Nikita Krushchev

A man who dares to waste one hour of time has not discovered the value of life.

Do you love life? Then do not squander time, for that's the stuff life is made of.

The art of life is the avoidance of pain.

Never resist temptation; try all things and hold fast to that which is good.

Talk slowly—think quickly.

Be not simply good, be good for something.

While you struggle to remember small kindnesses, try to forget small faults.

Love, like a cough, cannot be hidden.

A crowd is extraordinarily credulous and open to influence. An individual is much less easy to influence.

Appearance overpowers
even the truth.

Whoever controls the
language and the images,
controls the game.

Never mind whom you praise, but
be very careful whom you blame.

Edmund Gosse

The grand achievement of the present age is the diffusion of superficial knowledge.

People seem happy to content
themselves with what is commonplace.

**Let him that would move the world
first move himself.**

Robert Frost

Practical politics consists in ignoring facts.

**You can tell the ideals of a nation
by its advertisements.**

Where does a dream go after you've dreamt it?

Yesterday is but today's memory, and tomorrow is today's dream.

Kahlil Gibran

Magic happens when you believe in it.

The golden rule is moderation in all things.

Nothing in excess.

Victory is a thing of the will.

Who cannot limit himself can never be able to write.

Accept the limitations of your mind.

Moderation in temper is always a virtue, but moderation in principle is always a vice.

Get the
facts first.
You can
distort
them later.
    Mark Twain

All is flux, nothing is stationary.

All things change, nothing perishes.

No single thing abides; but all things flow.

There is nothing permanent except change.

The source of man's unhappiness is his ignorance of nature.

The best way to keep one's word is never to give it.

Napoleon Bonaparte

The marriage of the soul with nature makes the intellect fruitful; the fruit it bears is imagination.

To live in accordance with nature is to live in accordance with virtue.

Everything in excess is opposed to nature.

Live according to nature.

The secret to creativity is knowing how to hide your sources.

Albert Einstein

Beauty is eternity gazing at itself in a mirror.

Wonders are many, and none is more wonderful than man.

The decisive question for man is: is he related to something infinite or not?

Your prayer must be for a sound mind in a sound body.

Enjoy what you can, endure what you must.

Goethe

We should draw, from our own selves, images powerful enough to deny our own nothingness.

We must be our own saviors.

Science without religion is lame. Religion without science is blind.

The peace we are seeking so eagerly has been there all the time.

No doctrine, however high, however true, can make men happy until it is translated into life.

Minds rust.

Time is a great teacher, but it kills all its pupils.

When your life begins to go downhill there's always somebody there greasing the road.

What the world needs is dirtier fingernails and cleaner minds.

Old men give advice to console themselves for no longer being in a position to set bad examples.

First, learn the meaning of what you say, and then speak.

Epictetus

It is said that the rings of Saturn are composed of lost airline baggage.

There's nothing wrong with the average person that a good psychiatrist can't exaggerate.

Anyone can hold the helm when the sea is calm.

Don't go on appearances—there is nothing more deceiving.

Ugliness and beauty are both very much in the eye of the beholder.

Late is better than never.

The bigger they come, the harder they fall.

Choose to beg and you can't be a chooser.

Never promise more than you can perform.

Publius Syrus

Sometimes the cure is worse than
the disease.

Don't judge a book by its cover unless
you are learning to read.

Sometimes, if your basket
can hold all your eggs, it's
worth the risk.

Early to bed and early to rise makes a
man healthy, wealthy, wise...but
perhaps a little grumpy first thing.

Money is said to be the root of all evil...usually by those with little or no money.

A friend in need is still
a friend.

Haste makes waste.

Never trust the advice of a
man in difficulties.

Aesop

Mind your p's and q's but
let your a's and b's run wild.

Misery loves company.

He who
laughs last
didn't
understand
the joke.

If it's not one thing it's another
and if it's neither then it's something
altogether different.

**It's never too late to mend your
ways—or anything else that's broken.**

No pain, no gain, the choice is
yours to take.

Live and let live.

A place for everything and
everything in its place.

**The hardest victory is the
victory over self.**

Open your arms to change,
but don't let go of your values.

To stand still on the summit of perfection is impossible, in the natural course of things, what cannot go forward slips back.

The heart has its reasons which reason does not understand.

The best, and sternest, teacher is experience.

A great many open minds should be closed for repairs.

Look carefully, even if it is painful, at what is actually there in front of you.

When people talk,
listen completely.
Most people never
listen.

Ernest Hemingway

Perhaps, after everything else has been tried, honesty is the best policy.

Focus

The harder you work, the harder it is to surrender.

Winning is a habit. Unfortunately, so is losing.

Adversity makes a man wise, not rich.

Some rejoice in victories—others rejoice when strawberries grow.

Enthusiasm means the difference between mediocrity and accomplishment.

Enthusiasm is infectious, stimulating and attractive. Show enthusiasm and others will love you for it.

Old age is like a runaway train— once you're aboard there's nothing you can do about it.

Many would rather be ruined by praise than saved by criticism.

See possibilities— they're always there, although sometimes they're hiding.

We tend
to get
what we
deserve,
not
always
what we
expect.

Every problem has within it the seeds of its own solution.

We struggle with the complexities and avoid the simplicities.

No man is above the law and no man is below it.

Do what you can, with what you have, where you are.

Work hard at work worth doing.

Do the right thing, or the wrong thing. The worst thing you can do is nothing.

Speak softly and carry a big stick; you will go far.

To do evil is never justified, even on the grounds of expediency.

We can all be extraordinarily patient provided we get our own way in the end.

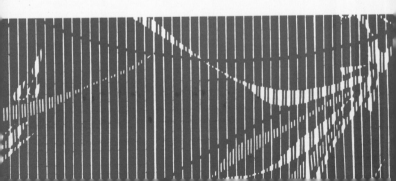

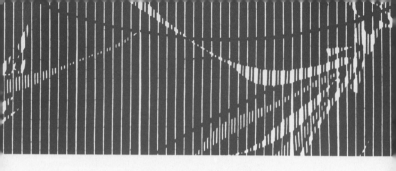

You may have to fight a battle more than once to win it.

Sometimes you have to be evasive.

If you can't stand the heat, get out of the kitchen.

Study men, not historians.

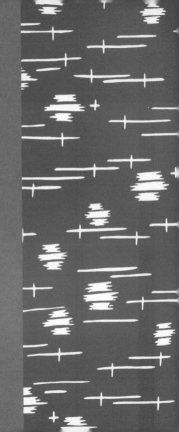

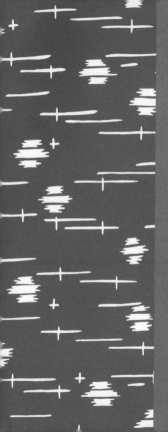

Being too good is apt to be uninteresting.

We must have strong minds if we are to accept facts as they are.

True friendship is a
plant of slow growth.

If you can't convince, confuse.

'Tis better to be alone than in bad company.

It's what you learn after you know it all that counts.

Character is what you are; reputation is what others think you are.

Don't measure yourself by what you have accomplished, but by what you should have accomplished with your ability.

Don't let what you can't do interfere with what you can do.

Be more
concerned
with your
character
than with
your
reputation.

Some people explore the universe while others get lost going to the shops.

Experience is what you get when you were expecting something else.

If you don't have time to do it right you must have time to do it over.

Do not regret growing older. It is a privilege denied to many.

Time is nature's way of keeping everything from happening at once.

What the world really needs is more love and less paperwork.

Most people, if they lived their lives again, would make the same mistakes only sooner.

To divide one's life by years is to tumble into a trap set by our own arithmetic.

Abundance, like want, ruins many.

The afternoon knows what the morning never suspected.

After three days without reading,
talk becomes flavorless.

Do not push the river, it will flow by itself.

All things good
to know are
difficult to
learn.

Danger and delight
grow on one stalk.

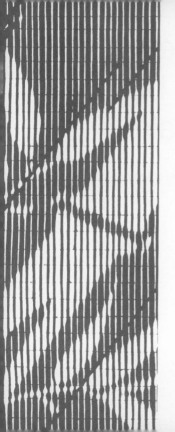

Ask a lot, but take what is offered.

Do not be in a hurry to tie what you cannot untie.

Don't think there are
no crocodiles because
the water is calm.

Avoid the evil, and it will avoid you.

Bad is never good until worse happens.

**The beginning is the half of
every action.**

Be happy while you're living, for you're a long time dead.

Ask for advice from the experienced rather than the learned.

The best armor is to keep out of range.

Be on your guard against a silent dog and still water.

Better to be ill spoken of by one before all than by all before one.

Better to light a candle than to curse the darkness.

Advice is least heeded when most needed.

Between saying and doing, many a pair of shoes is worn out.

God will be present, whether asked or not.

Beware of a man of one book.

The big thieves hang the little ones.

By asking for the impossible,
obtain the best possible.

Call on God, but row away from
the rocks.

By learning you will teach; by teaching you will learn.

Complain to one who can help you.

Confessed faults are half mended.

When love is not madness, it is not love.

Deceive the rich and powerful if you will, but don't insult them.

The deeper the sorrow
the less tongue it has.

Deliberate often—decide once.

Do not protect yourself by a fence,
but rather by your friends.

All sunshine makes the desert.

Do not
lengthen the
quarrel while
there is an
opportunity
of escaping.

Don't stand in a place of danger trusting in miracles.

Don't be too sweet lest you be eaten up; don't be too bitter lest you be spat out.

Don't fall before you're pushed.

Don't run too far, you will have to return the same distance.

Don't speak unless you can improve on the silence.

Eat and drink with your relatives;
do business with strangers.

**Even a fool is thought wise if he
keeps silent, and discerning if
he holds his tongue.**

Every animal knows more than you do.

After the game, the king and the pawn go back into the same box.

Examine what is said,
not him who speaks.

Every path has its puddle.

Don't shake the tree when the
pears fall off themselves.

The eyes believe themselves; the ears believe other people.

Experience is the comb that nature gives us when we are bald.

First deserve, and then desire.

Everyone thinks his own
burden is heaviest.

First secure an
independent income,
then practice virtue.

Get what you can and keep what
you have; that's the way to get rich.

A fool finds no pleasure in understanding but delights in airing his own opinions.

Gratitude is the heart's memory.

A half-truth is a whole lie.

A handful of patience is worth a bushel of brains.

A little pot boils easily.

Learn to
listen or
your
tongue will
keep you
deaf.

A man's first care should
be to avoid the reproaches
of his own heart, only
then should he worry
about escaping the
censures of the world.

Never trust the man who tells you all his troubles but keeps from you all his joys.

Man has responsibility, not power.

Make sure to be in with your equals if you're going to fall out with your superiors.

Nature, time and patience are the three greatest physicians.

One does evil enough when one does nothing good.

Never trouble trouble till trouble troubles you.

No revenge is more honourable than the one not taken.

A razor may be
sharper than an axe,
but it cannot cut wood.

One should be just as careful in choosing one's pleasures as in avoiding calamities.

Patience is a bitter plant, but it has sweet fruit.

A thousand regrets do not cancel one debt.

You often meet your destiny on the road you take to avoid it.

A single conversation with a wise man is better than ten years of study.

Tell me and I'll forget. Show me, and I may not remember. Involve me, and I'll understand.

The shortest answer is doing.

Since the house is on fire let us warm ourselves.

There is a pinch of madness in every great man.

Measure a thousand times
and cut once.

Never stand when you
can sit, or sit when you can
lie down.

Even a clock that does not work is right twice a day.

Every road has two
directions.

Goodness speaks
in a whisper,
evil shouts.

Be slow in choosing
a friend, but slower
in changing him.

Enjoy yourself. It's later than you think.

Published in 2000 by
Sourcebooks, Inc
1935 Brookdale Road, Suite 139
Naperville IL 60563

Text © David Baird 2000
Design concept: Broadbase
Design: Susannah Good

Printed and bound in Spain

MQ 10 9 8 7 6 5 4 3

ISBN: 1-57071-525-4